SHAKE, TAP, AND PLAY A MERRY TUNE

Making and Using Musical Instruments with Early-Childhood Learners

by Tania K. Cowling

Fearon Teacher Aids
Simon & Schuster Supplementary Education Group

About the Author

Tania Cowling, a specialist in music education for young children and a former columnist for *Early Childhood Music Newsletter*, teaches music classes and conducts workshops for preschool and day-care centers in Florida. *Shake, Tap, and Play a Merry Tune* is a collection of musical instrument ideas from her many years of teaching.

Editors: Marilyn Trow and Sue Mogard
Copyeditor: Kristin Eclov
Design: Terry McGrath
Cover Design: Marek/Janci Design
Cover and Inside Illustration: Janet Skiles
Production: Rebecca Speakes

ISBN-0-86653-949-2

Printed in the United States of America

1.9 8 7 6 5 4 3 2

CONTENTS

ACTIVITY CARDS FOR CHILDREN

CHANTS, SONGS, AND GAMES

TO THE TEACHER

*T*HERE ARE many positive reasons for making and using musical instruments in the classroom: sensory-motor skills are developed (such as eye-hand coordination and general gross-motor strength), auditory awareness is enhanced as children learn to discriminate between the high/low, slow/fast, and loud/soft sounds, and memory skills are improved through copycat games using different sound patterns.

While store-bought instruments may be exciting to children at first, they fail to keep the children's attention for long periods of time. The making of musical instruments offers children fun, creative, hands-on experiences with materials, encourages pride of ownership that peaks attention spans, and is musically educational as well. *Shake, Tap, and Play a Merry Tune* teaches young children the fun of learning by doing. Children are involved in every step needed to make the musical instruments:

♪ bringing materials from home

♪ helping to set up the project area

♪ making the instruments with minimal adult supervision

♪ playing the instruments together in the classroom

MATERIALS

Many simple instruments may be made and enjoyed by children with minimal adult intervention. The materials are simple: bamboo, wood, seashells, coconut shells, beads, and, of course, household items. Inviting parents to donate materials will encourage children to feel a part of the preparation and will greatly increase their interest in each musical instrument. Send the parent letter provided on page 7 home at the beginning of the year so items may be collected throughout the school year. Always stress safety—all collected materials must be safe and clean for the children to work with and enjoy. Keep the materials in a central cupboard in the classroom. This will also enable the children to help with setup and cleanup, adding to their sense of responsibility and capability in the classroom.

Suggestions for Using Instruments

After making each musical instrument, discuss the possible uses for it. Encourage a few moments of free experimentation, then invite the children to try to use their instruments to add rhythmic sounds to songs or chants. Introduce games that use the instruments, such as walking quickly or slowly to a drum beat. A second instrument may be introduced to encourage the children to compare the similarities and differences between the two. Finally, gather the children and the instruments together to form a classroom band.

FORMAT

Shake, Tap, and Play a Merry Tune is divided into three easy-to-follow sections:

Teacher's Guide to Making and Using Instruments

This section provides background information about each of the different types of instruments, clearly describes the steps for making each musical instrument, and suggests effective teaching strategies for using the instruments in the classroom.

Activity Cards for Children

This reproducible section offers pictorial directions for making the musical instruments described in the teacher's section. Step-by-step directions are provided for the children to follow to make each instrument. However, the activity cards introduce only the steps the children can do independently or with minimal adult participation. Accompanying action words clearly state the process the children are to complete. This encourages word association and beginning reading skills. Reproduce and laminate the cards at the beginning of the year so they will be ready for use when needed. Display the cards near a project table for easy reference by the children as they make their instruments.

Chants, Songs, and Games

This section contains chants, songs, and games that feature the instruments the children make. Include other favorites—yours and the children's as well. Although specific musical instruments are featured with each activity, these are only suggestions.

The following elements of music may be experienced through instruments:

> *Timbre*—the quality of sound that characterizes each instrument and makes it distinct from all other instruments. A triangle, for example, never sounds like a drum.
>
> *Tempo*—the speed at which music is played.
>
> *Crescendo* and *Decrescendo*—a gradual increase and decrease in level of sound.
>
> *Pitch*—the differences in high and low tones.
>
> *Rhythm*—refers to the beat and time the music is played in (2/4, 3/4, 4/4, and so on).

I invite you to shake, tap, and play a merry tune with your children. Discover together how much fun learning can be!

Tania K. Cowling

ear Parent,

This year we will be creating musical instruments in our classroom. We need your help in saving items that might be used to make musical instruments.

aluminum foil	newspapers
aluminum pie tins	pencils
camera film containers (35 mm)	pipecleaners
	plastic beads (medium and large)
cardboard tubes (paper towel and toilet tissue)	plastic bleach bottles (well rinsed)
	plastic milk jugs
chopsticks	popcorn kernels
cigar or cheese boxes (wooden)	popsicle sticks
	ribbons
clay flowerpots	rubber bands
coconut shells	sandpaper
coffee cans with plastic lids	seashells
cone-shaped paper cups	shoebox lids
elastic thread	small margarine tubs with lids
heavy cardboard	small plastic juice jugs with handles and lids
heavy yarn, string, and cord	
heavy-duty paper plates	small tomato sauce cans (tape the edges)
jingle bells (medium and large)	
large buttons (2" or larger)	soup cans (tape the edges)
large juice cans (tape the edges)	stickers
	thimbles
large nails (for adult use only)	thread spools
medium-size vegetable cans (tape the edges)	vinyl tape
	wallpaper paste (wheat paste)
metal bottle caps	waxpaper or cellophane
metal cookie tins	wooden beads (medium and large)
metal paper clips	wooden dowel sticks
metal washers	wooden paint stirrers (new)

Please send to school any of these items that you are willing to donate. For safety reasons, please wash all objects and cover any possible sharp edges with masking tape. We appreciate your help!

Sincerely,

SHAKE, TAP, AND PLAY A MERRY TUNE © 1992 FEARON TEACHER AIDS

TEACHER'S GUIDE TO MAKING AND USING INSTRUMENTS

Bells

BELLS have been important throughout history. They have been used to warn people, announce special happenings, and tell the time. Bells were first used to make music in the Middle Ages. Musical bells (called cymbala or bell chimes) were hung from a rack and struck with a mallet. Later, larger sets of bells were put together to make a carillon. Today, electronic organs and carillons are often used to imitate the sounds of bells.

Featured Chants, Songs, and Games

Getting Started

Ask the children to recall if they have ever heard bells ringing. Help the children come up with a list of places where bells can be heard, such as doorbells, church bells, or school bells. Write the list on chart paper, even though the children may not be able to read the words. It is important for children to see the relationship between the written and the spoken word. Encourage the children to predict which items in the classroom will ring when struck with a wooden spoon or pencil. Invite different children to strike various objects in the classroom with a wooden spoon or pencil to check their guesses.

FLOWERPOT BELLS

Materials *(Makes 1 Instrument)*

3 different sizes of clay flowerpots

3 1-foot lengths of heavy cord

wooden spoon or pencil

board

hammer (adult use only)

nails (adult use only)

Directions

1. Help children tie a large knot in one end of each length of heavy cord.

2. Ask children to thread one cord through the hole in the bottom of a flowerpot, leaving the knot on the inside. Follow the same process for the other pots.

3. Have an adult volunteer nail the cord of each flowerpot bell securely to a board. Place the board on two chairs allowing the bells to hang between them.

4. Children then gently tap the pots with a wooden spoon or pencil.

Challenge!

Ask the children to predict which pot will make the highest sound when struck with the wooden spoon or pencil. (The smallest pot will make the highest sound.)

TIN CAN BELL

Materials *(Makes 1 Instrument)*

soup can (remove one end)

empty thread spool

2 large buttons

glue

yarn or string

hammer

large nail (adult use only)

stickers and vinyl tape

tempera paint

paintbrushes

newspaper

masking tape

Directions

1. Have an adult volunteer punch a hole in the end of the soup can using a hammer and a large nail. Cover the edges of the can with masking tape.

2. Have children tie two buttons together using one end of the yarn or string. Provide help as needed (young children will not be able to tie without adult supervision).

3. Have an adult volunteer place a small piece of tape around the end of the yarn. Help the children thread the taped end of the yarn through the hole in the can from the inside out and then through an empty thread spool.

4. Help children spread glue on the bottom of the spool and then push the spool tightly against the top of the can to make a handle.

5. Lower the string slightly in the can until the buttons hang about one-third of the way down.

6. Help children tie a large knot in the string close to the top of the spool.

7. When the spool is secure and the glue is dry, children can decorate the can and spool with stickers, vinyl tape, or tempera paints. Have children wear protective smocks when painting. (Do not cover the entire surface of the can with stickers or vinyl tape as this will deaden the sound.)

8. Children hold the can by the spool and shake it back and forth until the buttons inside the can hit the sides, making a tinkling sound.

Challenge!

Encourage students to experiment with making different sounds by shaking the tin can bells at different speeds, hitting them against a variety of surfaces, varying the amounts and types of decorations, and so on. Provide students with a variety of sizes of tin can bells to play with. Encourage the discovery that the size of the bell changes the sound.

WATER BELLS

Materials *(Makes 1 Instrument)*

5 clear water glasses
(all the same size and
at least 6 inches tall)

ruler

water

metal spoon

numbered cards
from 1 to 5

Directions

1. Help children line up five clear water glasses in a row. Place a numbered card (1 to 5) next to each glass.

2. Help children pour water into each glass as follows. Use a ruler to help you.

1 inch in glass 1	4 inches in glass 4
2 inches in glass 2	5 inches in glass 5
3 inches in glass 3	

3. Tap each glass lightly with a metal spoon. Ask the children to name the numbered glass with the highest pitch and then name the glass with the lowest pitch. Encourage the children to order the glasses by pitch from lowest to highest.

Challenge!

Show the children how to play a simple or favorite song, such as "Happy Birthday to You." Then invite the children to create their own simple songs using the five water bells. Provide opportunities for the children to share their songs with one another in class. The water bells may be "tuned" by adding or removing water. Help the children discover that adding more water produces a lower sound and removing water produces a higher sound. Some children may wish to add more glasses of water to complete the scale.

Drums & Tambourines

DRUMS are among the oldest and most commonly used instruments. Drums were originally made from hollow logs and beaten with the hands to create different rhythms for ancient dances. Today, drums are a part of every orchestra and band. Tambourines are also fun to play and can be used in bands of all sizes. Drums and Tambourines add rhythm to all types of music in countries around the world.

Featured Chants, Songs, and Games

Getting Started

Ask the children if they have ever heard a drum before. Encourage the children to come up with a list of places where drums can be heard. Write the list on chart paper, even though the children may not be able to read the words. It is important for children to see the relationship between the written and the spoken word.

Clap several simple rhythms for the children to imitate and follow. Invite the children to make up clapping rhythms of their own as well. Then tap some rhythms on a desk or the floor using a pencil. Encourage the children to use pencils to repeat the rhythms. Praise all the children's efforts. Be sensitive to the fact that some children may have problems with auditory discrimination. Ask the children what instrument in a band or orchestra is used to help keep all the other instruments on the beat.

BONGO

Materials *(Makes 1 Instrument)*

2 half-gallon or gallon clean plastic bleach bottles (cut the tops off—the same amount from each bottle—and then tape the cut edges)

vinyl tape in various colors

stickers

stapler

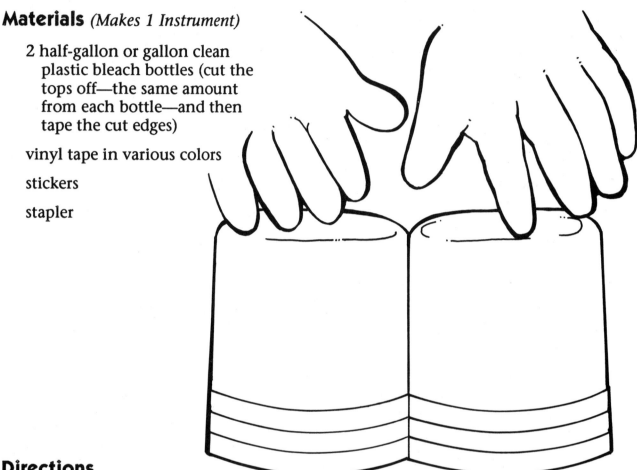

Directions

1. Have an adult volunteer staple two bleach bottles together side by side for each child.

2. Children can then decorate the bottles with strips of colorful tape and stickers.

3. Children turn the bottles upside down and tap the bottom of the bottles with their hands. They may also enjoy sitting on the floor with the bongos between their legs, playing both drums rhythmically.

Challenge!

Play a simple rhythmic pattern for the children. Then encourage the students to try and repeat the rhythm on their drums. Praise all the children's efforts. Continue this activity with several other patterns. Invite interested students to create rhythmic patterns of their own.

MARGARINE TUB TOM-TOM

Materials *(Makes 1 Instrument)*

small margarine tub with a lid

wooden dowel stick (about 6" x 1/2")

2 large wooden or plastic beads

5-inch length of heavy string or yarn

paper punch

knife (adult use only)

stickers

masking tape

Directions

1. Have an adult volunteer punch a small hole in one side of the margarine tub with a paper punch.

2. Invite the children to decorate the margarine tub and dowel stick with colorful stickers.

3. Place a small piece of masking tape around one end of the string. Help children thread the heavy string or yarn through the hole in the margarine tub.

4. Help children tie one bead securely to the end of the string inside the tub. They then tie another bead on the opposite end of the string.

5. Have an adult cut a small X in the side of the tub—about 45° from the hole. Be sure to do the cutting out of reach of the children.

6. Help children slide the wooden dowel in the slit as a handle and then place the lid on the plastic tub.

7. Help children hold the dowel stick upright between the palms of their hands. They then rub their hands together to hear the beads beat on the drum.

Challenge!

Encourage each child to practice rubbing his or her hands together at different speeds to change the rhythm of the drum. Challenge students to find other ways to play the tom-tom, too.

MARGARINE TUB TAMBOURINE

Materials *(Makes 1 Instrument)*

small margarine tub with lid

6 metal bottle caps

3 metal washers

3 pipecleaners

permanent felt-tip markers

paper punch

hammer (adult use only)

large nail (adult use only)

Directions

1. For safety reasons, this activity may be more appropriate for older children. Have an adult volunteer carefully punch a hole in the center of six bottle caps using a large nail and a hammer. Do this in advance of the activity.

2. Give each child a margarine tub to decorate using permanent felt-tip markers.

3. Show children how to string a bottle cap, a washer, and another bottle cap (in this order) on each pipecleaner. Encourage the children to follow the same procedure. Provide close adult supervision, watching carefully that younger children do not place bottle caps or washers in their mouths.

4. Have an adult volunteer punch two holes about an inch apart in the side of the margarine tub using the hammer and nail or a paper punch. Do this out of the reach of children.

5. Have children thread the ends of a pipecleaner into the holes, leaving the bottle caps and washer to the outside of the plastic tub.

6. Have children twist the ends of the pipecleaner together inside the margarine tub.

7. Help the children repeat steps 3–5 with the other pipecleaners, spacing them evenly around the margarine tub.

8. Once the tambourines are finished, children can hold the margarine tubs in their hands and shake or tap them against their thighs.

Challenge!

Play some music. Encourage students to experiment with shaking or tapping their tambourines to the music.

DRUM NECKLACE

Materials *(Makes 1 Instrument)*

coffee can with both ends removed (paint with enamel spray paint)

2 plastic lids to fit the coffee cans

3-foot length of ribbon or yarn

stickers in various colors

hammer (adult use only)

large nail (adult use only)

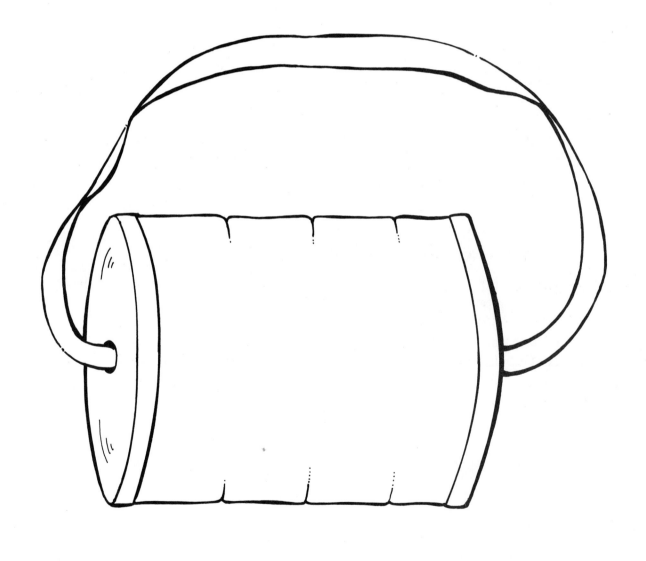

Directions

1. Have an adult volunteer punch a hole in the middle of each plastic lid using a nail and hammer. This should be done in advance of the activity.

2. Help children thread the ribbon through the hole in one lid (from the inside out).

3. Have an adult volunteer help each child tie a knot at the end of the ribbon inside the lid.

4. Have children thread the other end of the ribbon through the hole in the second lid (from the outside in).

5. Have an adult volunteer help the children tie a knot on the inside of the other lid.

6. Place both lids on the coffee can. The length of ribbon should hang outside the can like a "necklace."

7. Encourage children to decorate the can with colorful stickers.

8. Children can hang the cans around their necks and march around the classroom tapping the lids with both hands. Provide close adult supervision. Invite children to remove the drums from around their necks as soon as they lose interest.

Challenge!

Invite the children to experiment hitting the drums with different parts of their hands (fingers, palms, nails, sides) to create a variety of sounds. The children can also use pencils and other objects as well. See who can make the loudest sound, the softest sound, the most unusual sound, and so on.

PAPER-PLATE TAMBOURINE

Materials *(Makes 1 Instrument)*

heavy-duty paper plate

3–5 jingle bells

3–5 five-inch lengths of elastic thread or yarn

paper punch

tempera paint

paintbrushes

felt-tip markers, crayons, glitter, or other decorations

glue

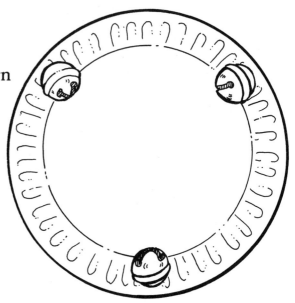

Directions

1. For safety reasons, this activity may be more appropriate for older children. Have an adult volunteer punch three to five evenly spaced holes around the outside rim of the paper plate.

2. Invite children to decorate their plates with paint, felt-tip markers, or crayons. Glitter or other decorations may be added as well.

3. Have an adult volunteer help the children thread each length of elastic thread or yarn through a jingle bell. Provide close adult supervision, particularly for younger children.

4. Have an adult volunteer help the children tie the bells to the holes in the plate.

5. Children can hold the plate in their hands and shake it. They may also tap the tambourines against their thighs.

Challenge!

Encourage the children to create a variety of sounds by hitting the tambourines with different parts of their bodies—heads, elbows, knees, and so on. Sing the song "Heads and Shoulders, Knees, and Toes," but instead of tapping the body parts mentioned in the song, lightly tap the tambourine.

Snare Drum

Materials *(Makes 1 Instrument)*

metal cookie tin with lid

metal paper clips (about 20)

cardboard circle (cut slightly larger
   than the diameter of the tin)

masking tape

glue

stickers and glitter

tempera paint

paintbrushes

unsharpened pencil or chopstick

newspaper

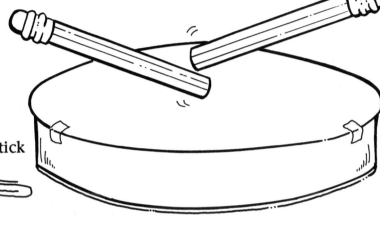

Directions

1. Have children remove the lid from the empty cookie tin.

2. Children can then decorate the outside of the cookie tin with paint, glitter, and stickers.

3. Have children paint the cardboard circle for extra color.

4. Have children turn the cookie tin upside down and spread paper clips evenly on the recessed bottom of the tin.

5. Have an adult volunteer help the children place the cardboard circle over the bottom of the tin. The cardboard should not touch the paper clips.

6. Have an adult volunteer help the children secure the cardboard circle to the bottom of the tin with masking tape.

7. Children can use an unsharpened pencil or chopstick to tap the cardboard.

Challenge!

Encourage the children to use other materials besides paper clips to see what other sounds may be produced. Help children discover which materials make the most interesting sounds.

TRIPLE CAN DRUM

Materials *(Makes 1 Instrument)*

large juice can (spray paint in
a bright color)

medium-size vegetable can
(spray paint in a bright color)

small tomato sauce can (spray
paint in a bright color)

heavy vinyl tape

stickers

masking tape

spray paint

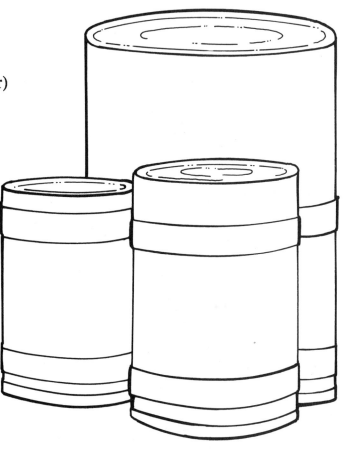

Directions

1. Help children place the three cans together with the bottoms facing
   up. Tape around the tops and bottoms of the cans to secure them
   together. Be sure all the can edges are covered with masking tape.

2. Have children decorate the cans with stickers.

3. Children can tap the cans one at a time with their fingers to produce
   different sounds.

Challenge!

Invite the children to add other size cans to their drum sets. Encourage
the children to guess why the different cans make different sounds.

Rhythm Blocks

RHYTHM BLOCKS are some of the simplest forms of percussion instruments. Rhythm blocks have changed very little through time, in material or in sound. Rhythm blocks are generally made of wood to produce distinct, unique sounds. Percussion sections of orchestras and bands use different types of rhythm blocks to create special sound effects.

Featured Chants, Songs, and Games

Getting Started

If possible, show the children several sets of rhythm blocks. Ask how sounds might be made with the blocks. Encourage the children to experiment making sounds with the instruments. Challenge the children to name items in the classroom that might make similar sounds. (Have some of the materials for making rhythm blocks displayed on a project table in the classroom.)

CHINESE WOOD BLOCKS

Materials *(Makes 1 Instrument)*

wooden cigar box (or oblong cheese box)

8-inch length of clothesline or heavy cord

drill (adult use only)

keyhole saw (adult use only)

sandpaper

wood stain or shellac (adult use only)

paintbrush

drumstick or mallet

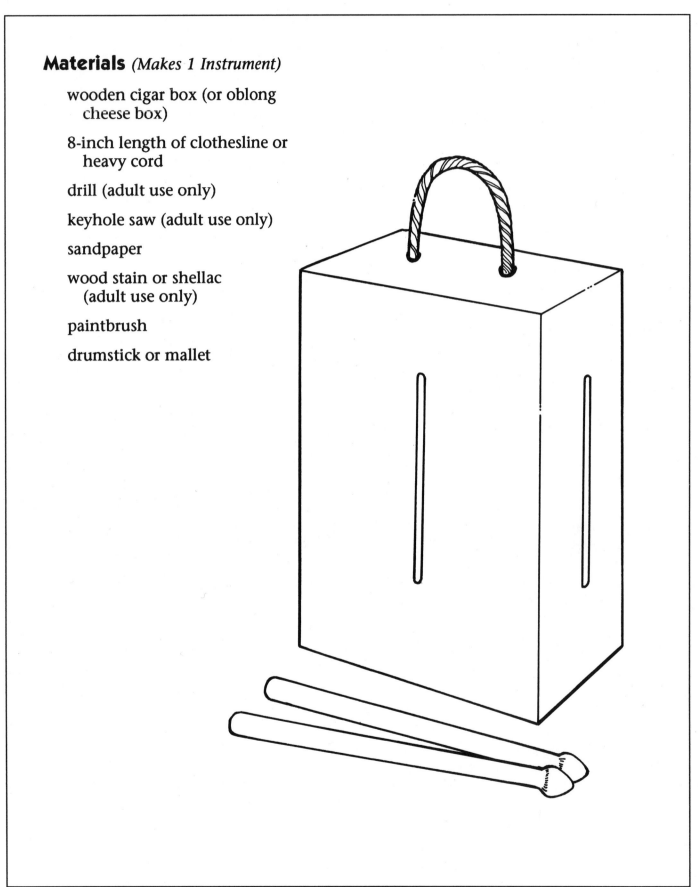

Directions

1. Stand the cigar box on end. Have an adult volunteer drill a 1/4″ hole approximately two inches from the top edge of the box and midway between the sides on each of the four faces. Flip the box over and repeat the process.

2. Have an adult volunteer use a keyhole saw to make a 1/4″ wide slit to connect the holes on each of the four sides of the box.

3. Have an adult volunteer drill two smaller holes on one end of the box.

4. Help children sand all cut edges.

5. Have children string heavy cord through the two holes in the end of the box—with the ends toward the inside of the box.

6. Have an adult volunteer help children tie a knot in the cord on each end.

7. Have an adult volunteer stain or shellac the box (paint will muffle the sound) in a well-ventilated area away from the children.

8. Children hold the wooden block by its handle and strike the block with a drumstick or small mallet. (The sound produced is similar to galloping horses and tramping feet.)

Challenge!

Encourage the children to experiment making a variety of different levels of sound—(p) soft, (mf) moderate, and (ff) very loud. Then help the children make up stories that incorporate sound effects that may be produced with the wooden blocks.

COCONUT CLAPPERS

Materials *(Makes 1 Instrument)*

coconut shell (cleaned and
   cut in half)

sandpaper

tempera paint

paintbrushes

paint smocks

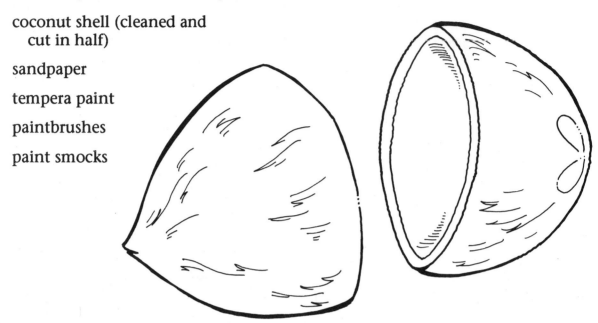

Directions

1. Help the children sand the outside of the coconut until the surface becomes somewhat smooth. Discuss what happens when different amounts of pressure are used to sand the coconut.

2. Children can then paint the coconut with tempera paint. Be sure the children wear paint smocks.

3. Holding one coconut half in each hand, children can tap the cut edges together to create unique, hollow-wood sounds. They may also enjoy tapping the rounded edges together to create a different sound.

Challenge!

Encourage children to guess which animal makes a sound like a coconut clapper (horse). Invite the students to use their clappers to make sounds like a horse—walking slowly, galloping, and finally, standing still. If appropriate, bring the students outside to an open area and challenge the students to gallop slowly in a large circle while tapping their coconut clappers.

DOWEL BOARD

Materials *(Makes 1 Instrument)*

5 wooden dowel sticks (1/2" x 5")

sandpaper

new wooden paint stirrer
  (or other thin strip of wood)

carpenter's wood glue

varnish (adult use only)

paintbrushes

metal or plastic thimble
  (or a dowel stick)

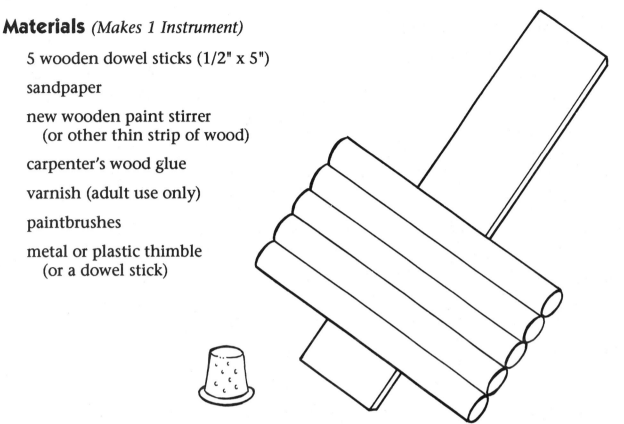

Directions

1. Help children sand the ends of the dowel sticks until the surfaces are smooth.

2. Help children place and glue the dowel sticks crosswise along the flat surface of the paint stirrer.

3. Have children glue between the dowel sticks for added strength as well.

4. After the glue is dry, have an adult volunteer varnish the sticks. Be sure to varnish a safe distance from the children and in a well-ventilated area.

5. Have children place a thimble on their thumbs or fingers and use downward strokes to brush over the dowel sticks to make washboard sounds.

Challenge!

Cut the dowel sticks in different lengths. Invite the children to predict if the sounds will vary on sticks of different lengths.

SANDPAPER BLOCKS

Materials *(Makes 1 Instrument)*

2 blocks of wood (2" x 4" x 6")

sandpaper

tempera paint

paintbrushes

2 rectangles of sandpaper (4" x 8")

heavy-duty stapler

2 empty thread spools

glue

paint smocks

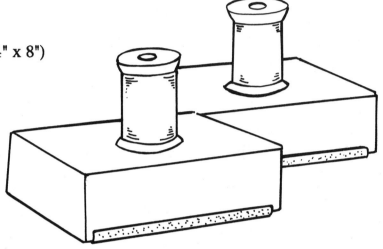

Directions

1. Show the children how to sand the edges of the blocks of wood.

2. Have children paint the blocks in bright colors. Remind the children to wear paint smocks.

3. Help children glue a spool on the center of one side of each wood block to serve as a handle. Allow the glue to dry over night.

4. Have an adult volunteer staple a rectangle of sandpaper to the opposite side of the blocks. Be sure to use the heavy-duty stapler a safe distance away from the children.

5. Encourage the children to tap the blocks together to make loud claps, or slide the sandpaper sides together to make shuffling sounds.

Challenge!

Invite children to create different rhythms or sounds using the sand blocks. Encourage the students to experiment—tapping the blocks together, sliding the sandpaper sides together in long strokes, short strokes, and so on.

Shakers

SHAKERS are unique percussion instruments used widely in music with a Latin American flavor. Shakers have been found in the artifacts of ancient Maya, Inca, and Aztec civilizations. A common Latin American shaker is the maraca made from dried gourds. Today, shakers are made from a variety of materials and used in a many types of music where a lively beat is needed.

Featured Chants, Songs, and Games

Getting Started

If possible, play some lively Latin American music for the children. Encourage the children to listen for the different percussion sounds. Ask them how they think the shaker sounds might be made. Show children a shaker, such as a maraca. Invite the children to take turns making sounds with it. Then ask the children to predict what might be inside the shaker.

CASTANETS

Materials *(Makes 1 Instrument)*

    1" x 6" strip of heavy cardboard

    string or yarn

    2 metal bottle caps

    hammer (adult use only)

    nail (adult use only)

    felt-tip markers

    tempera paint

    paintbrushes

    masking tape

Directions

1. For safety reasons, this activity may be more appropriate for older children. Have an adult volunteer punch a hole in the middle of each bottle cap using a hammer and a nail. Be sure to use the hammer and nails out of reach of the children.

2. Invite children to use markers or tempera paint to decorate the cardboard strips.

3. Then have an adult volunteer punch a hole an inch from each end of the cardboard strip using the hammer and nail.

4. Have children place a bottle cap face down over one of the holes in the cardboard strip—lining up the hole in the strip with the hole in the cap.

5. Place a small piece of masking tape around the end of the string. Then help the children thread the string through the holes. Provide close adult supervision with younger children whenever small objects are being used to create instruments.

6. Help the children tie a knot in the string on both sides of the bottle cap.

7. Help the children repeat steps 3–5 on the other end of the cardboard strip.

8. Help the children fold the cardboard strip in half with the bottle caps on the inside.

9. Children hold the folded end of the cardboard strip in one hand and click the bottle caps together by squeezing the cardboard.

Challenge!

Invite the children to practice squeezing the castanets together to make different sounds. Play simple rhythms for the students to practice on their castanets. The speed at which the children are able to play the castanets will increase with practice.

Jingle Bracelet

Materials *(Makes 1 Instrument)*

12-inch length of rawhide string
   or ribbon

large plastic or wooden beads

3 large jingle bells

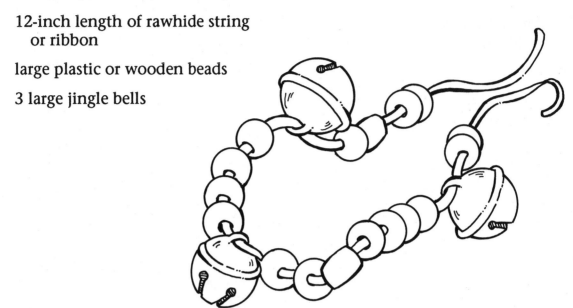

Directions

1. Help children string the beads and bells on the rawhide or ribbon. This activity should be closely supervised. Be careful that young children do not place the beads in their mouths.

2. Help the children tie the ends of the string or ribbon together in a knot to form a bracelet.

3. Children can hold the bracelet in their hands and shake it. They might also try tapping the bracelets against their thighs to make jingle-tap sounds!

Challenge!

Play some music. In an open area of the classroom, encourage the children to wear their jingle bracelets and creatively move to the music. Point out the many different sounds created by the variety of movements. Invite interested students to experiment with wearing the bracelets on their ankles, too.

JUG SHAKER

Materials *(Makes 1 Instrument)*

6-inch plastic juice jug with handle and lid

jingle bells

medium-sized plastic or wooden beads (in bright colors)

stickers

glue

heavy-duty tape

Directions

1. Help children fill the jug half full of bells and beads. Closely supervise this activity to be sure young children do not place beads or bells in their mouths.

2. Help children place glue along the inside edge of the lid.

3. Have an adult volunteer screw the lid on the jug.

4. Wrap heavy-duty tape around the lid to reinforce it for safety reasons.

5. Children can then decorate the jug with stickers.

6. Have children hold the jug by its handle and shake. They can also try shaking the jug up and down and side-to-side to make a variety of shaker sounds!

Challenge!

Fill the jug with different amounts and combinations of bells and beads. Invite children to predict the differences in the sounds they will hear. List the children's ideas on chart paper, even though the children may not be able to read the words. It is important for children to see the relationship between the written and the spoken word. Encourage the children to compare the different sounds produced.

Popcorn Maraca

Materials *(Makes 1 Instrument)*

plastic 35-mm film container
(cut a slit in the lid)

popsicle stick (wash in a little
bleach if brought from home)

popcorn kernels

glue

musical stickers

markers

spray paint (adult use only)

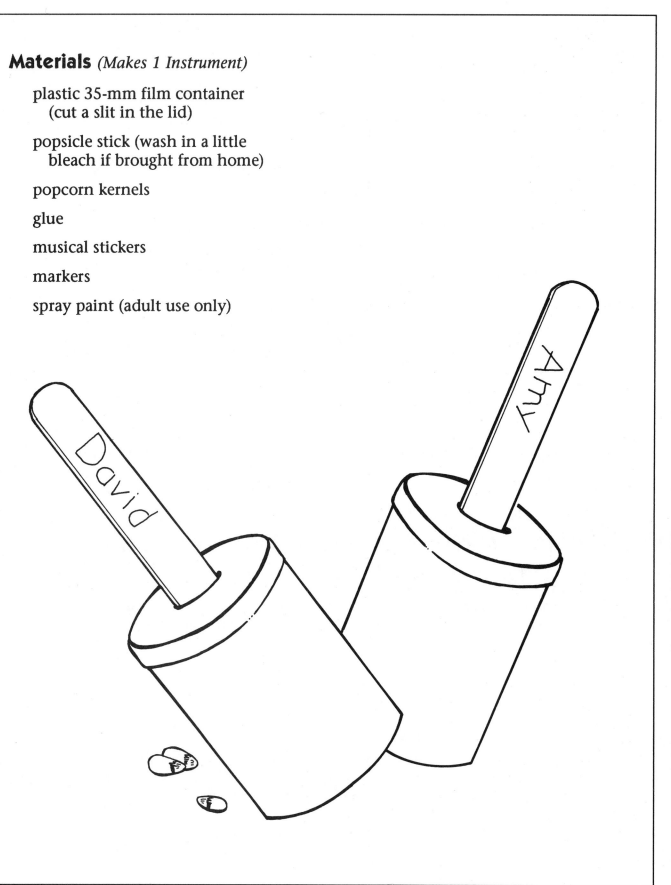

Directions

1. Help children fill a film container about one-fourth full of popcorn kernels. Closely supervise this activity to be sure young children do not put the kernels in their mouths.

2. Help children place a little glue along the inside edge of the film container lid.

3. Have an adult volunteer close the lid tightly on the container.

4. Have an adult volunteer write each child's name on a popsicle stick. Older children may choose to write their own names.

5. Children can then slide the stick through the slit in the lid of the film container.

6. Spray paint each maraca in a well-ventilated area a safe distance away from the children.

7. When the paint dries, encourage the children to decorate their maracas with stickers.

8. Encourage the children to hold the sticks firmly and then shake their maracas to make wonderful sounds.

Challenge!

Provide other materials, such as rice and beans, and encourage the children to fill other film containers with these materials. Have children compare the sounds.

Seashell Shaker

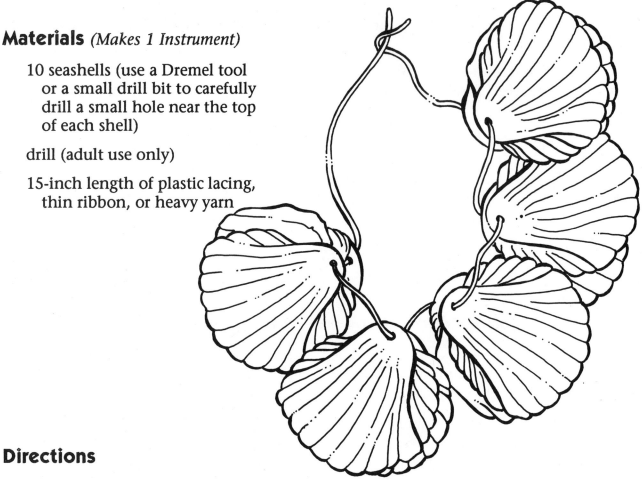

Materials *(Makes 1 Instrument)*

10 seashells (use a Dremel tool or a small drill bit to carefully drill a small hole near the top of each shell)

drill (adult use only)

15-inch length of plastic lacing, thin ribbon, or heavy yarn

Directions

1. Have an adult volunteer drill small holes in the top of each shell prior to this activity.

2. Children can string the seashells together—front-to-front in pairs (like clamshells).

3. Help the children tie the ends of the lacing together in a knot.

4. Have children hold the shaker by the lacing and shake vigorously. They may also tap shakers against their thighs to create other shaker sounds.

Challenge!

Encourage the children to string the shells back-to-back or front-to-front to see if different sounds may be created. Play several different types of music, such as marching band or polka, and encourage the children to shake their seashell shakers to the music.

Woodwinds

WOODWINDS are instruments that make sounds when air is blown into or across a mouthpiece. Early woodwinds were hand carved from wood and played by traveling folk minstrels. Today, flutes, piccolos, oboes, clarinets, bassoons, English horns, and other woodwinds are an important part of most orchestras and bands.

Featured Chants, Songs, and Games

Getting Started

Invite the children to sing a favorite tune. Give each child a sheet of paper. Show the children how to roll the papers into tubes. Then have the children sing into the tubes. Encourage the children to discuss what happens. Introduce the term *vibrating*. Ask the children if they can feel the paper vibrating as they sing. Point out that most woodwinds are also shaped like tubes.

MUSICAL KAZOO

Materials *(Makes 1 Instrument)*

toilet-tissue tube

4" x 4" square of colorful
   cellophane (or waxpaper)

rubber band

felt-tip markers, colored pencils,
   or stickers

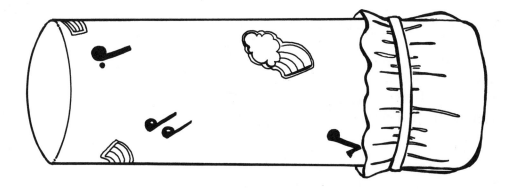

Directions

1. Children can use markers or colored pencils to decorate the tube, or decorate with stickers, if desired.

2. Have an adult volunteer help the children stretch cellophane over one end of the tube and secure it with a rubber band. Closely supervise children when working with rubber bands.

3. Children then hum into the open end of the tube. (The special kazoo sound is made when the cellophane vibrates on the opposite end of the tube.)

Challenge!

Suggest that the children use a paper punch to punch two or more holes in the sides of the tubes. Then have children play the kazoos and compare the sounds. Some children may experiment by covering one or more holes with their fingers as they hum.

RECORDER

Materials *(Makes 1 Instrument)*

paper-towel tube
  (about 12 inches long)

cone-shaped drinking cup

aluminum foil

tape

circle stickers
  (or paper circles and glue)

scissors

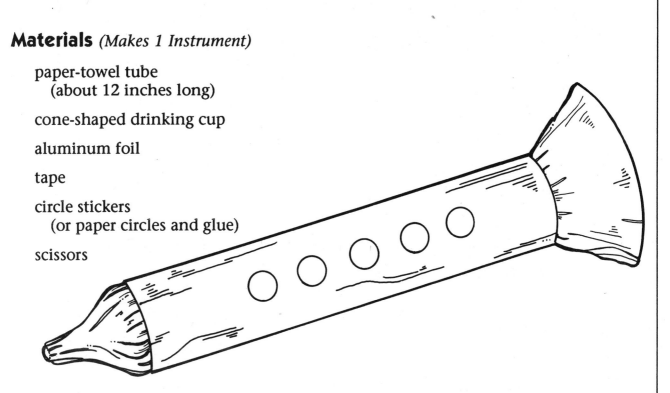

Directions

1. Help children cover the tubes with foil.

2. Have an adult volunteer help the children make a mouthpiece out of foil. Leave an opening in each end of the mouthpiece.

3. Have an adult volunteer cut off the pointed end of the cone-shaped cup.

4. Help children cover the cone with foil.

5. Help children tape the cone to the bottom end of the tube.

6. Show children how to arrange round stickers in a line along the top of the tube to represent "keys" on a recorder.

7. Finally, have children hum into the mouthpiece and pretend to press the "keys" on the top of the tube.

Challenge!

Provide a variety of different-size tubes and cups. Invite the children to use the materials to make other recorders and then compare the sounds.

Other Instruments

THERE ARE a wide variety of string and percussion instruments. These instruments are some of the oldest instruments around. Guitars and banjos, for example, were played by traveling minstrels, cowboys, and other people on the move. Their sounds invited people to gather for listening or for dancing. Today, young and old alike are still entertained by guitars and banjos, as well as electric guitars and other synthesized instruments.

Featured Chants, Songs, and Games

Getting Started

If possible, show the children a banjo or guitar (or a picture of a banjo or guitar). Ask the children if they know how sounds are made on these instruments. Play a recording of banjo and guitar music. Encourage the children to share how the music makes them feel. Show the children a cymbal, too. Invite the children to experiment with making different sounds with the cymbal.

Box Banjo

Materials *(Makes 1 Instrument)*

2 shoebox lids that are the same size (cut a 2" x 4" rectangular section from the center of one lid)

rubber bands of various widths

glue

stickers

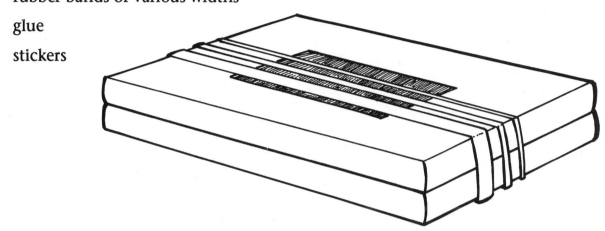

Directions

1. Help children glue the edges of the shoebox lids together. Allow the glue to dry over night.

2. Invite children to decorate the lids with stickers.

3. Have an adult volunteer help the children stretch the rubber bands (at least four different widths) across the longer opening of the lid.

4. Children can pluck the rubber bands like strings on a banjo and create a variety of different sounds. Caution children to pluck the rubber bands gently so they won't break. Immediately discard any broken pieces.

Challenge!

Invite the children to pluck, strum, and pick the rubber bands to create long, short, and other interesting sound effects. Ask the children to predict how the sounds are made. Then have each child pluck one of the rubber bands and quickly place a finger on the vibrating band to see what happens. Help the children discover that thin, tight bands produce high sounds and thick, loose bands produce low sounds.

CYMBALS

Materials *(Makes 1 Instrument)*

2 aluminum pie tins

toilet-tissue tube

2 brad fasteners

permanent felt-tip markers

tempera paint

paintbrushes

scissors (adult use only)

paper punch

paint smocks

newspaper

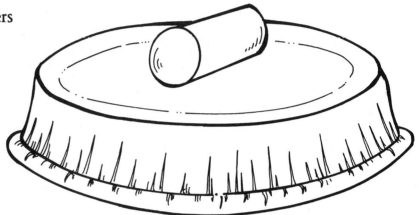

Directions

1. Have an adult volunteer use scissors to punch a hole in the center of each pie tin. Be sure to punch the holes out of reach of the children.

2. Invite children to use permanent markers to decorate the pie tins.

3. Have an adult volunteer carefully cut the toilet-tissue tube in half and then use a paper punch to poke a hole in the middle of the side of each tube.

4. Children can then paint the tubes with tempera paint. Be sure the children wear paint smocks.

5. Help children attach each tube to a pie tin by inserting a brad fastener through the holes in the pie tins and tubes.

6. Have children hold the cymbals by the tube handles and then hit the edges of the pie tins together.

Challenge!

Encourage the children to practice hitting the cymbals together in different ways to create interesting sounds. Praise all the children's efforts.

ACTIVITY CARDS
FOR CHILDREN

FLOWERPOT BELLS

1. Tie

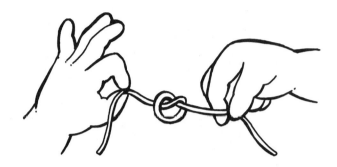

2. Thread

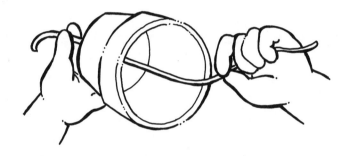

3. Play

TIN CAN BELL

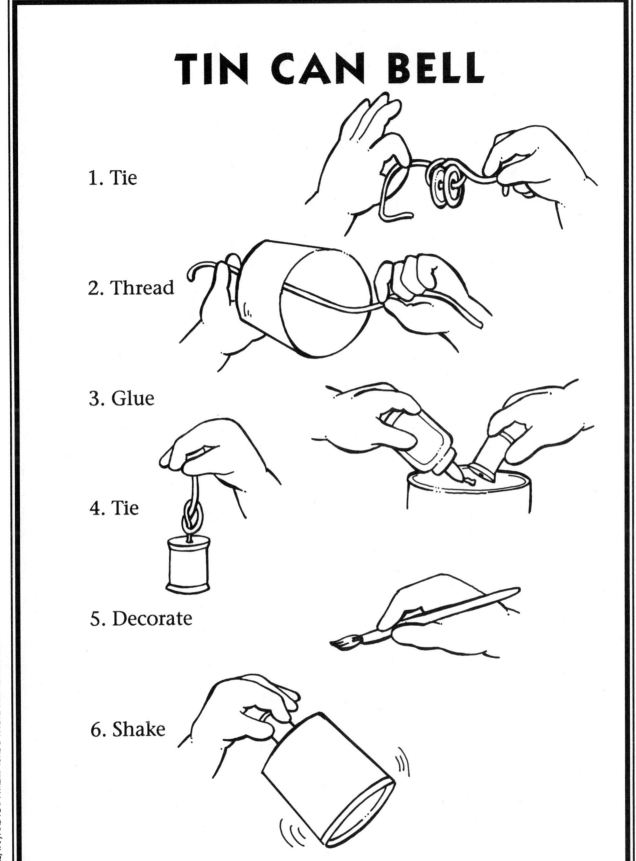

1. Tie

2. Thread

3. Glue

4. Tie

5. Decorate

6. Shake

SHAKE, TAP, AND PLAY A MERRY TUNE © 1992 FEARON TEACHER AIDS

WATER BELLS

1. Line Up

2. Pour

3. Play

BONGO

1. Decorate

2. Play

MARGARINE TUB
TOM-TOM

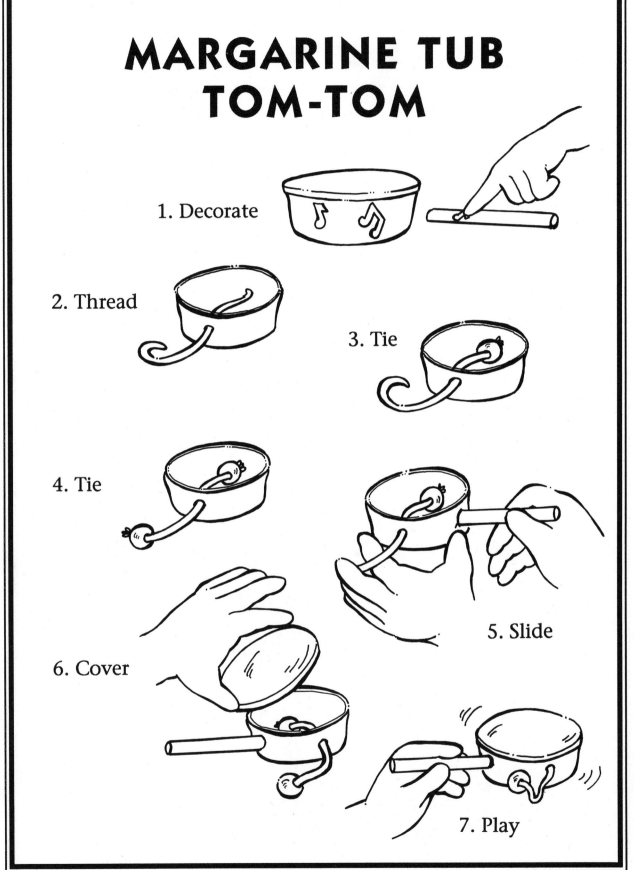

1. Decorate

2. Thread

3. Tie

4. Tie

5. Slide

6. Cover

7. Play

SHAKE, TAP, AND PLAY A MERRY TUNE © 1992 FEARON TEACHER AIDS

MARGARINE TUB TAMBOURINE

1. Decorate

2. String

3. Thread

4. Twist

5. Play

DRUM NECKLACE

1. Thread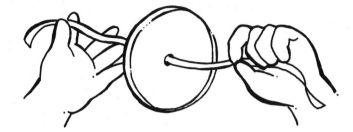

2. Tie

3. Thread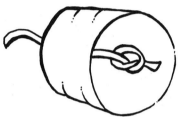

4. Tie

5. Decorate

6. Play

SHAKE, TAP, AND PLAY A MERRY TUNE © 1992 FEARON TEACHER AIDS

PAPER-PLATE TAMBOURINE

1. Decorate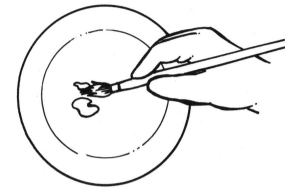

2. Thread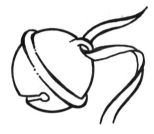

3. Tie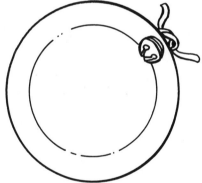

4. Play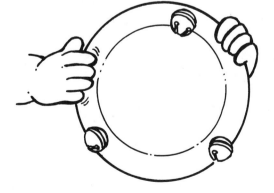

SNARE DRUM

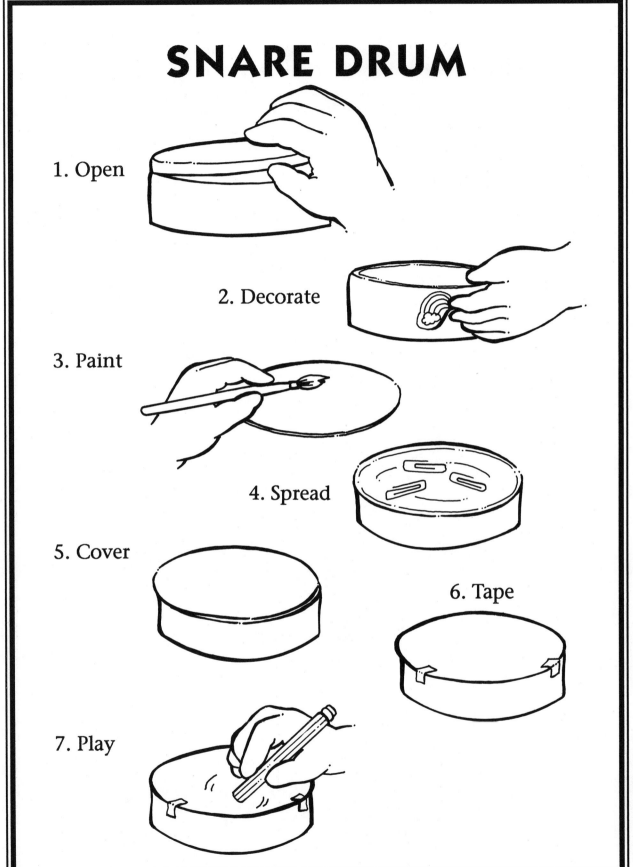

1. Open

2. Decorate

3. Paint

4. Spread

5. Cover

6. Tape

7. Play

SHAKE, TAP, AND PLAY A MERRY TUNE © 1992 FEARON TEACHER AIDS

TRIPLE CAN DRUM

1. Line Up

2. Decorate

3. Play

CHINESE WOOD BLOCKS

1. Sand

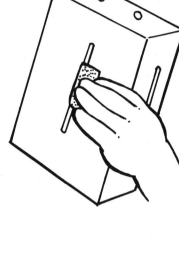

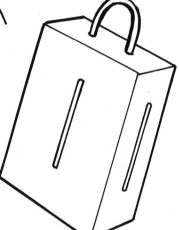

2. String

3. Tie

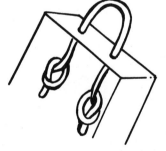

4. Play

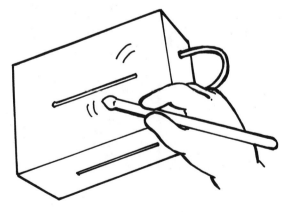

SHAKE, TAP, AND PLAY A MERRY TUNE © 1992 FEARON TEACHER AIDS

COCONUT CLAPPERS

1. Sand

2. Paint

3. Play

DOWEL BOARD

1. Sand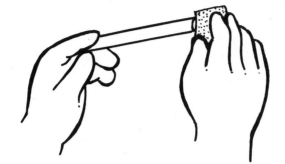

2. Glue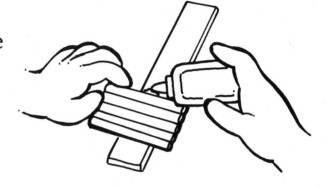

3. Glue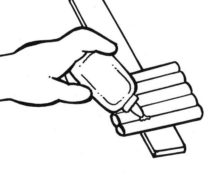

4. Play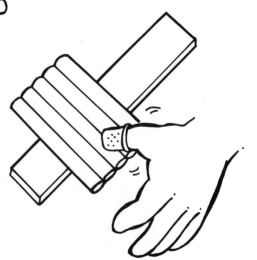

SANDPAPER BLOCKS

1. Sand

2. Paint

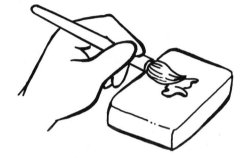

3. Glue

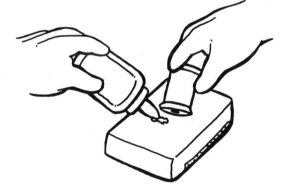

4. Play

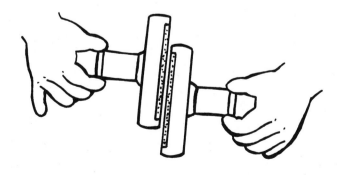

CASTANETS

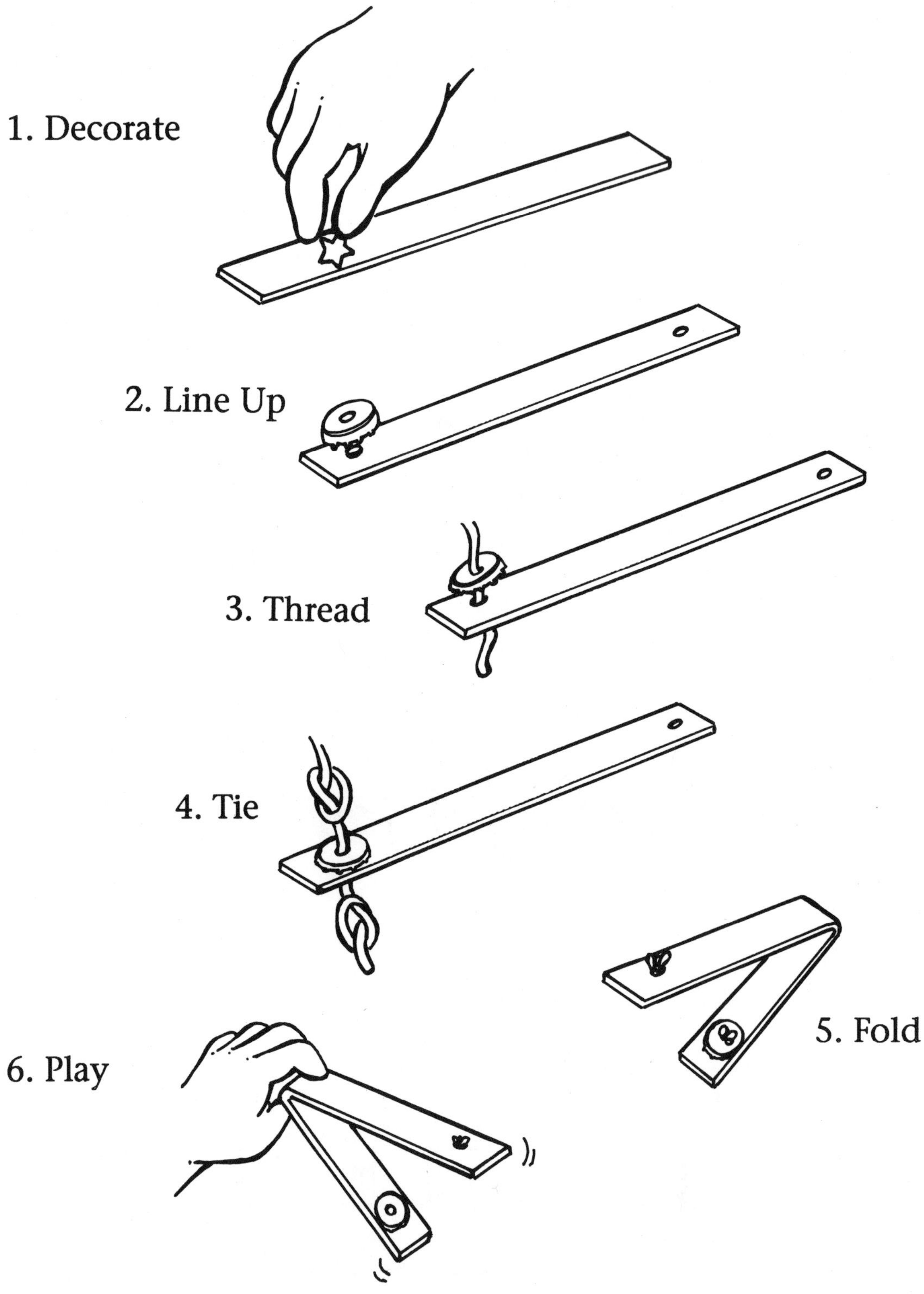

1. Decorate

2. Line Up

3. Thread

4. Tie

5. Fold

6. Play

SHAKE, TAP, AND PLAY A MERRY TUNE © 1992 FEARON TEACHER AIDS

JINGLE BRACELET

1. String

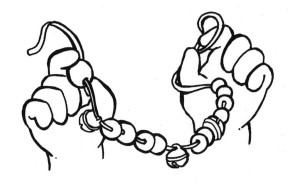

2. Tie

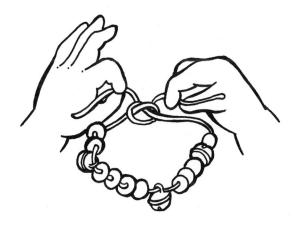

3. Play

SHAKE, TAP, AND PLAY A MERRY TUNE © 1992 FEARON TEACHER AIDS

JUG SHAKER

1. Fill

2. Glue

3. Decorate

4. Shake

SHAKE, TAP, AND PLAY A MERRY TUNE © 1992 FEARON TEACHER AIDS

POPCORN MARACA

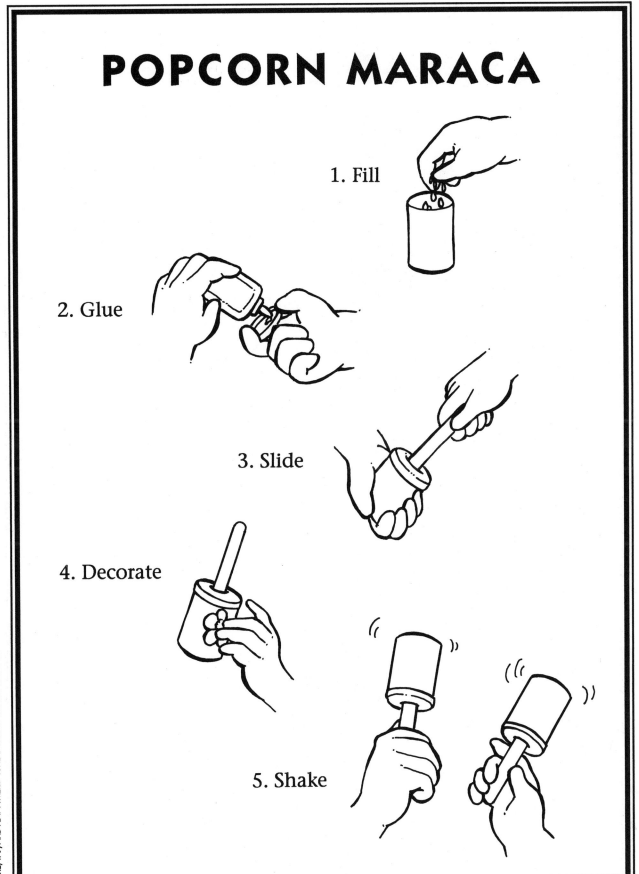

1. Fill

2. Glue

3. Slide

4. Decorate

5. Shake

SEASHELL SHAKER

1. String

2. Tie

3. Shake

MUSICAL KAZOO

1. Decorate

2. Stretch

3. Play

RECORDER

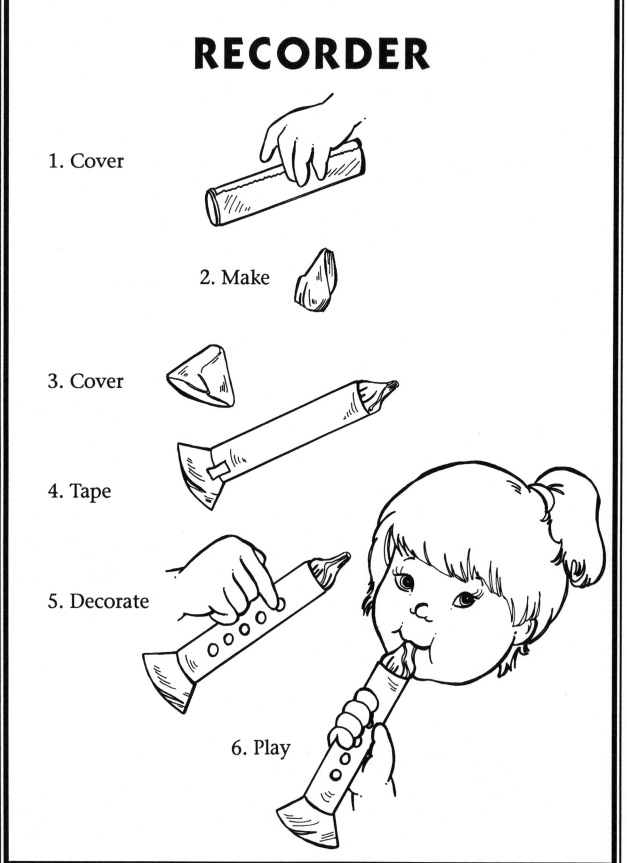

1. Cover

2. Make

3. Cover

4. Tape

5. Decorate

6. Play

SHAKE, TAP, AND PLAY A MERRY TUNE © 1992 FEARON TEACHER AIDS

BOX BANJO

1. Glue

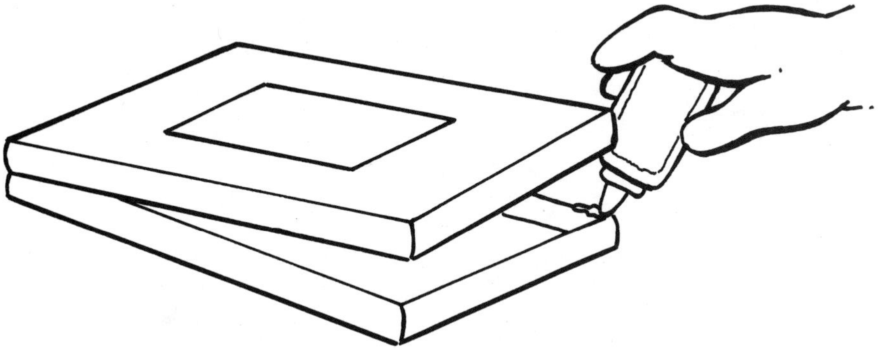

2. Decorate

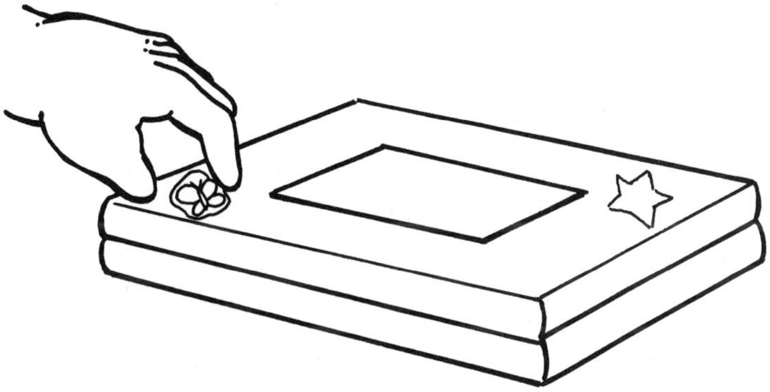

3. Stretch

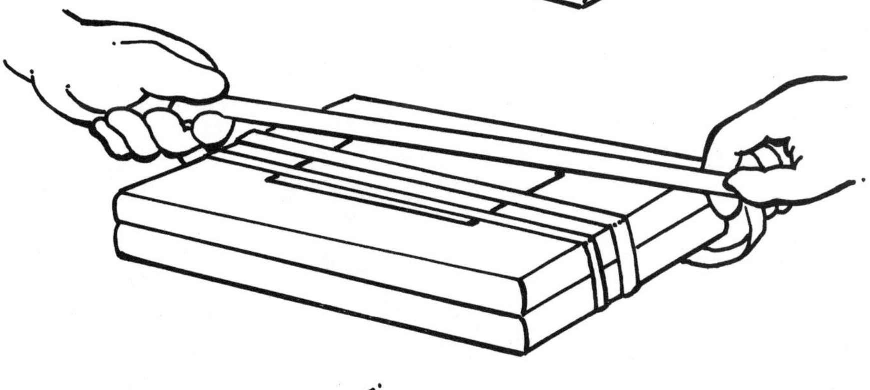

4. Play

CYMBALS

1. Decorate

2. Paint

3. Play

CHANTS, SONGS, AND GAMES

Chants

Teddy Bear

Suggestions: Recite the poem and then play it rhythmically with instruments.

Featured Instruments: Drums, Rhythm Blocks, Shakers

Teddy bear, teddy bear, turn around.
Teddy bear, teddy bear, touch the ground.
Teddy bear, teddy bear, shake a tune.
Teddy bear, teddy bear, I love you!

Miss Mary Mack

Suggestions: Play instruments each repeated word.

Featured Instruments: Drums, Rhythm Blocks, Shakers

Miss Mary Mack, Mack, Mack,
All dressed in black, black, black
With silver buttons, buttons, buttons
Up and down her back, back, back.
She asked her mother, mother, mother
For fifteen cents, cents, cents
To see the elephants, elephants, elephants
Jump the fence, fence, fence.
They jumped so high, high, high,
They touched the sky, sky, sky,
And they never came down, down, down
Until the Fourth of July, July, July.

Songs

Await the Sound
(sung to the tune of "Farmer in the Dell")

Suggestions: Substitute the names of other instruments in the song and describe those instrument sounds.

Featured Instrument: Cymbals

The cymbals go crash, crash,

The cymbals go crash, crash,

At the end of a round, await the sound,

The cymbals go crash, crash.

The drums go boom, boom,

The drums go boom, boom,

At the end of a round, await the sound,

The drums go boom, boom.

The sandpaper blocks go swish, swish,

The sandpaper blocks go swish, swish,

At the end of a round, await the sound,

The sandpaper blocks go swish, swish.

The flowerpot bells go ding, ding,

The flowerpot bells go ding, ding,

At the end of a round, await the sound,

The flowerpot bells go ding, ding.

Classroom Playtime Band

(sung to the tune of "It's a Small World")

Suggestions: Play instruments as suggested in the song. Insert other instruments and directions in place of rhythm blocks and tambourines.

Featured Instruments: Tambourines, Rhythm Blocks

Verses

> *Play your rhythm blocks to the count of four.*
> *One, two, three—ee, four—one, two, three—ee four.*
> *Oh, the rhythm sounds fine, and you're marching in time*
> *In our classroom playtime band.*
>
> *Tambourines sound grand in our playtime band.*
> *Tap and shake so fast and again so slow.*
> *Oh, the rhythm sounds fine, and you're marching in time*
> *In our classroom playtime band.*

Chorus

> *Time to play your instrument.*
> *March in place with your instrument.*
> *Keep the beat with your instrument*
> *In our classroom playtime band.*

Join in the Game *(sung to the tune of "Let Ev'ryone Clap Hands Like Me")*

Suggestions: Play shakers as directed in the song.

Featured Instruments: Shakers

Let ev'ryone play (name an instrument) like me (shake, shake).
Let ev'ryone play (name an instrument) like me (shake, shake).
Come on and join in the game.
You'll find that it's always the same (shake, shake).

La Raspe

Suggestions: Create rhythm patterns for playing instruments.

Featured Instruments: Tambourines, Castanets

With clicking of castanets and jingle of tambourine,
All work of the day forgot, and dancing tonight is queen.
We're dancing a dance from old Mexico. La, la, la, la, la, la
Our steps light and gay, and our hearts aglow. La, la, la, la, la, la.

Music Is in the Air *(sung to the tune of "Row, Row, Row Your Boat")*

Suggestions: Play instruments as directed in the song.

Featured Instruments: Drums, Rhythm Blocks, Shakers

Play it loud,
Play it soft,
Rhythm everywhere.
Play it slow,
Play it fast,
Music is in the air!

Oh, What Fun!
(sung to the tune of "Jingle Bells")

Suggestions: Mark the beat with bells.

Featured Instruments: Bells

Jingle bells, jingle bells,
Jingle all the way.
Oh, what fun it is to be
In a classroom band, hurray!

Old MacDonald's Band
(sung to the tune of "Old MacDonald Had a Farm")

Suggestions: Play instruments as directed in the song. Substitute names and descriptions of other instruments as well.

Featured Instruments: Maraca

We are members of a band.
Shake, shake, shake, shake, shake
And in this band we have a maraca.
Shake, shake, shake, shake, shake
With a shake, shake here and a shake, shake there,
Here a shake, there a shake, everywhere a shake, shake.
We are members of a band.
Shake, shake, shake, shake, shake.

Play in the Band
(sung to the tune of "Deck the Halls")

Suggestions: Substitute different instruments in the third stanza.

Featured Instruments: Bells, Drums, Rhythm Blocks, Jingle Bracelets

We are all musicians now.
Come listen to our song,
And play along.

We will play our instruments.
Just listen to each one.
It's lots of fun.

First we'll play the castanets (children holding castanets play in time as follows).
Click, click, click, click, click, click,
Click, click, click.
Let's all play together now (finish song with all instruments playing in time).

Use Your Instrument Today
(sung to the tune of "Twinkle, Twinkle Little Star")

Suggestions: Play instruments as directed in the song. Substitute the names and descriptions of other instruments as well.

Featured Instruments: Tambourines

Use your tambourines today
To help you sing and dance this way.
Jingle, jingle, tap, tap, tap,
Keep the rhythm with a shake and tap.
So play your tambourine today
To help you sing and dance this way.

Games

The Conductor Leads the Band

Featured Instruments: Drums, Rhythm Blocks, Shakers

Select one child to role-play a band conductor. Have the rest of the children stand together in groups according to the instruments they hold. Play some music and invite the "conductor" to stand in front, wave a baton in time to the music, and point to different groups of children to play. Provide opportunities for all children to role-play the conductor.

Follow Directions

Featured Instruments: Shakers

Shake your (instrument) to the right (shake, shake, shake).
Shake your (instrument) to the left (shake, shake, shake).
Shake your (instrument) above your head (shake, shake, shake).
Shake your (instrument) between your legs (shake, shake, shake).

Wave your (instrument) at a neighbor (wave, wave, wave).
Wave your (instrument) in a circle (wave, wave, wave).
Wave your (instrument) and run in place (wave, wave, wave).
Wave your (instrument) on your tip toes (wave, wave, wave).

Tap your (instrument) with your fingers (tap, tap, tap).
Tap your (instrument) and jump up and down (tap, tap, tap).
Tap your (instrument) with your knee (tap, tap, tap).
Tap your (instrument) sitting on the ground (tap, tap, tap).

Instrumental Chairs

Featured Instruments: Bells, Drums, Rhythm Blocks, Shakers, Woodwinds,
  and Other Instruments

Arrange chairs in a large circle. Place a bell, drum, rhythm block, or shaker on each chair. Invite the children to sit on the chairs and hold the instruments. Play some music. As the music begins, encourage the children "play" the instruments they hold. When the music stops, instruct the children to stand, put the instruments on the chairs, and move to different chairs. When the music begins once again, invite the children to play the new instruments.

Listen to the Beat

Featured Instruments: Drums, Rhythm Blocks, Shakers

Help the children form a large circle. Use drums, rhythm blocks, and shakers to give movement directions to the children. Explain to the children that only the beat will talk to them. Encourage children to listen to how fast the beat invites them to move. When the beat is slow, the children move slowly around the circle. When the beat is fast, the children move quickly, and so on. This is a good listening skills game for learning to recognize different rhythms.

Orchestrate a Story

Featured Instruments: Rhythm Blocks

Share the story *Three Billy Goats Gruff* with the children. Invite the children to use rhythm blocks to make each goat's hoof sounds as you tell about the goats crossing over the bridge. Suggest that children play the blocks softly for the smallest goat, louder for the medium-size goat, and very loud for the largest goat.

An Overture

Featured Instrument: Cymbals

Invite the children to listen to Tchaikovsky's "1812 Overture." The children will enjoy crashing cymbals together with this famous musical piece. Children may need to be cautioned to "crash" gently.

Play a Tune

Featured Instruments: Water Bells

Invite the children to use the numbered water bells to play the following simple tunes (and other tunes the children may wish to play as well).

"Three Blind Mice"
  3-2-1
  3-2-1
  5-4-4-3
  5-4-4-3

"Mary Had a Little Lamb"
  3-2-1-2-3-3-3
  2-2-2
  3-5-5
  3-2-1-2-3-3-3
  3-2-2-3-2-1

Record a Song

Featured Instruments: Kazoos, Recorders

Invite the children to hum a favorite song into their kazoos or recorders. Play songs for the children and encourage them to play along as well. Record the songs on a tape recorder and then play the tape back for the children's enjoyment!

Rhythm Card

Featured Instruments: Rhythm Blocks

Reproduce the following rhythm card for the children to use when playing their dowel boards or other rhythm instruments. Two short lines together signify two short sounds on the instrument. One long line directs the children to make one long sound.

"TWINKLE, TWINKLE, LITTLE STAR"

| | | | | | ——

| | | | | | ——

| | | | | | ——

| | | | | | ——

| | | | | | ——

| | | | | | ——

Shape Orchestra

Featured Instruments: Bells, Drums, Rhythm Blocks, Shakers, Woodwinds, and Other Instruments

Cut large shapes (triangles, circles, squares, rectangles) from construction paper to place on the floor. Assign a shape for each type of instrument. Then invite the children to stand on the shapes according to the instruments they select (all the children playing rhythm blocks stand on triangles, all the children playing bells stand on squares, and so on).

Play music with a definite beat. Conduct the music by calling out names of shapes or by showing a picture of a shape. Invite the children standing on the designated shapes to play in time with the music. Enjoy choosing more than one shape at a time and listening to the band "harmonize."

Tap Out Your Name

Featured Instruments: Rhythm Blocks

Have the children sit together in a circle. Go around the circle and call out each child's name. Then help the children tap out the syllables in their own and their classmates' names by shaking or tapping rhythm blocks once for each syllable. Older or more advanced children can add the last names, too.

Which Instrument Is This?

Featured Instruments: Bells, Drums, Rhythm Blocks, Shakers, Woodwinds, and Other Instruments

Select a child to be "it." Invite the child who is "it" to go behind a screen and play one instrument. Encourage the other children to listen carefully and try to identify the instrument being played. Select the child who first guesses correctly to become the next "it." Continue as long as the children show interest.